I Have a Stepfamily

by Colleen LeMaire

Illustrated by Marina Saumell

Dedicated to Jaime, my Stepmom support system. Our conversations mean more to me than you'll ever know. Stepmoms need someone who just "gets it," and you do. Each and every time. Thank you.

To Sue. You are the closest thing to a Stepmom I'll ever have. Thank you for our friendship. And you'll never be "too old" for me!

To the ladies at Stepmom Magazine, both readers and writers. Thank you for keeping me sane. I love you all.

To my parents. Thank you for showing me what a healthy and happy marriage looks like. I am proud to have one of my own now.

To Cassidy, who made me a Stepmom. From the moment we met, you have let me into your heart. I am so proud of the beautiful relationship we have, and I hope you never stop following your own head and your own heart.

Lastly, to my husband. Your patience for the world we are in amazes me. Thank you for picking me up when stepmotherhood knocks me down, and for being my prince charming in our modern day fairy tale. I love you so much.

Once upon a time, my Daddy met a beautiful girl.

He fell in love with her,

One magical day, my Dad asked her to marry him.
She said yes!

And she asked me to be
her flower girl in the wedding!

It was a wonderful wedding,
and she is now my Stepmom.

She lives with my Dad,
and when I am here, I get to spend time with her.

Her heart is so big she loves me
and my Dad as big as the sky!
And it makes me happy to see my Dad happy.
He's the best Dad ever, and deserves
a heart full of true love!

My Stepmom helps my Dad take care of me.

She helps give me my baths,
and makes sure no soap gets in my eyes!

She cooks me dinner,
and helps me eat healthy
so I grow big and strong like Dad!

My Stepmom loves to watch me learn.
She taught me how to write my name, and I learned how to make friends in our neighborhood by watching her do it.

Sometimes we disagree with each other, and every now and then that makes us mad! But we always forgive. We start and end each day with a smile and a kiss!

My Stepmom made our family complete.
She loves me and my Dad so much,
and we love her too!

She's a great parent to me, and never forgets to be my friend, too.

Sometimes we have special GIRLS ONLY playdates together, and my Stepmom and I do something extra fun, just me and her!

Sometimes she gives me
and my Dad special alone time, too.
I miss my Dad when I am not here,
and my Stepmom gives me and him special time
to be silly together.

MOVIE NIGHT

And other times, we do things as one big happy family. My favorite is family movie night in our pajamas!

About the Author

Colleen was catapulted into the world of parenting when she fell in love with a handsome single Dad. Like any parent or stepparent, she has experienced the trials and triumphs of raising a child over the years, and says the journey has brought her a level of happiness she didn't know existed.

She is a loving Stepmom to her six-year-old stepdaughter, who sparked her passion to create this series. Colleen currently lives in the Chicagoland area with her husband, whom she says makes the crazy ride of parenthood is all worth it.

To get the latest news and updates on the
"I Have" Children's Book Series,
check out www.facebook.com/ihavestories

© Copyright 2015 by Colleen LeMaire.

All rights reserved. No part of this publication may be reproduced, stored in a retrieval system, or transmitted, in any form or by any means, electronic, mechanical, photocopying, recording, or otherwise, without the written permission of the author.

Published by Colleen LeMaire
Printed in the United States of America.

Illustrated by Marina Saumell

ISBN: 978-1512215236

Made in the USA
Las Vegas, NV
19 January 2024

84596463R00024